Collins English Readers

Amazing Philanthropists

Level 3
CEF B1

Text by
Jane Rollason

Series edited by
Fiona MacKenzie

Collins

HarperCollins Publishers
77–85 Fulham Palace Road
Hammersmith London W6 8JB

10 9 8 7 6 5 4 3 2 1

Original text
© The Amazing People Club Ltd

Adapted text
© HarperCollins Publishers Ltd 2014

ISBN: 978-0-00-754504-9

Collins® is a registered trademark of
HarperCollins Publishers Limited

www.collinselt.com

A catalogue record for this book is available
from the British Library

Printed in the UK by Martins the Printers

MIX
Paper from
responsible sources
FSC C007454

www.fsc.org

◆ Contents ◆

◆ Introduction ◆

Collins Amazing People Readers are collections of short stories. Each book presents the life story of five or six people whose lives and achievements have made a difference to our world today. The stories are carefully graded to ensure that you, the reader, will both enjoy and benefit from your reading experience.

You can choose to enjoy the book from start to finish or to dip into your favourite story straight away. Each story is entirely independent.

After every story a short timeline brings together the most important events in each person's life into one short report. The timeline is a useful tool for revision purposes.

Words which are above the required reading level are underlined the first time they appear in each story. All underlined words are defined in the glossary at the back of the book. Levels 1 and 2 take their definitions from the *Collins COBUILD Essential English Dictionary* and levels 3 and 4 from the *Collins COBUILD Advanced English Dictionary*.

To support both teachers and learners, additional materials are available online at www.collinselt.com/readers.

The Amazing People Club®

Collins Amazing People Readers are adaptations of original texts published by The Amazing People Club. The Amazing People Club is an educational publishing house. It was founded in 2006 by educational psychologist and management leader Dr Charles Margerison and publishes books, eBooks, audio books, iBooks and video content, which bring readers 'face to face' with many of the world's most inspiring and influential characters from the fields of art, science, music, politics, medicine and business.

◆ THE GRADING SCHEME ◆

The Collins COBUILD Grading Scheme has been created using the most up-to-date language usage information available today. Each level is guided by a brand new comprehensive grammar and vocabulary framework, ensuring that the series will perfectly match readers' abilities.

		CEF band	Pages	Word count	Headwords
Level 1	elementary	A2	64	5,000–8,000	approx. 700
Level 2	pre-intermediate	A2–B1	80	8,000–11,000	approx. 900
Level 3	intermediate	B1	96	11,000–15,000	approx. 1,100
Level 4	upper intermediate	B2	112	15,000–19,000	approx. 1,700

For more information on the Collins COBUILD Grading Scheme, including a full list of the grammar structures found at each level, go to www.collinselt.com/readers/gradingscheme.

Also available online: Make sure that you are reading at the right level by checking your level on our website (www.collinselt.com/readers/levelcheck).

Alfred Nobel

◆ ◆ ◆

1833–1896

the man who created the Nobel Prize

I was a chemist and a businessman. My greatest invention was dynamite, and I made a large fortune from selling it around the world. Then, one day in Paris, five words changed my life forever.

◆ ◆ ◆

Although I was Swedish and was born in Stockholm, I grew up in St Petersburg in Russia. I arrived in the world in 1833, at a bad time for my family. My father had problems with his business and in the year that I was born, he lost all his money. He had a wife and three sons and he decided to start again in a new country. First he started a business in Finland, and then, when I was five, he moved to St Petersburg, leaving us behind in Stockholm.

My father was a great inventor, as well as a businessman. In northern Europe in those days, a lot of things were made out of wood. He invented clever new <u>tools</u> for making things out of wood, and created a successful business in his new Russian home. When I was nine years old, we were able to join him. My mother was very pleased that the family was back together, especially as she was going to have another baby. My brother, Emil, was born that year.

My father's company was called Nobel & Sons. It grew into a large engineering company, making all kinds of machines, from <u>steam engines</u> to early central heating. The <u>Industrial Revolution</u> was happening in Europe at this time. Machines could now make most things that humans had made by hand for centuries.

We lived in a comfortable wooden house in St Petersburg, but we were not rich. My brothers and I were educated at home by private teachers. We studied history, science and <u>literature</u>. As well as Swedish, which we spoke at home, we learnt to speak Russian, French, German and English. This helped me a lot later on when I <u>set up</u> companies around the world.

One of my favourite subjects was literature. I especially admired the English poet Shelley, with his love of <u>humanity</u> and peace, and his exciting political ideas. I wrote poems myself, but I was never satisfied with them and I always burned them. I shared my father's love of chemistry, and together we tried out new ideas. He also taught me how to be a good businessman.

When I was 17, in 1850, I left home to see some of the world. I spent a year in Paris, working with a famous French chemist. Then I went to the USA, where I studied the latest technology. Although I didn't go to university, I received an excellent education watching some of the world's best scientists. The long journey home to Europe across the

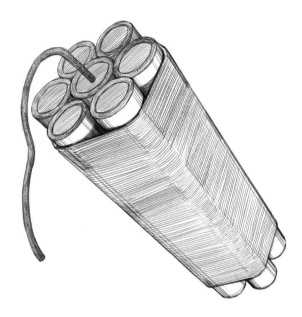

Atlantic gave me time to think about my future. What kind of business should I try? Over the last year I had become interested in <u>explosives</u>, which were very basic at that time.

My family was back in Sweden by now, and I joined them there. In 1863, I successfully created a new kind of explosive, using the chemical nitroglycerin, a kind of explosive liquid. Nobel & Sons was now based in Heleneborg in Sweden, where they tested new chemical recipes.

But one terrible day, an experiment went wrong. A huge explosion at the factory killed my younger brother Emil, and several of the company workers. It was a very sad day for the family, and we had a big decision to make. Should we sell the business and stop making explosives?

We decided to continue, but I moved away from Heleneborg. I set up my own factory near Hamburg in

Germany, calling it Alfred Nobel & Company. There was more bad luck, however. An enormous explosion destroyed the factory, and many of my workers were injured.

The explosives were not <u>stable</u>. I had to change the recipe. Nitroglycerin is very difficult to work with, and this had caused the explosions. In one experiment I added a new ingredient. The new mixture was still dangerous, but it was more stable than before. I called it 'dynamite'.

In the next few years I started new companies in the USA and Britain, making dynamite. I first showed my new product to the world in England. I set fire to sticks of dynamite and threw packets of dynamite off a <u>cliff</u>. The English decision-makers did not believe my new product was safe, however. Unfortunately, there was a big explosion near Liverpool in July 1869 caused by containers of nitroglycerin. After that, companies could not use or sell nitroglycerin, or move it from one place to another in England.

I could not get permission to open a dynamite factory in England. So I went to Scotland, where some businessmen helped me to set up The British Dynamite Company in April 1871, on the west coast. The factory was at Ardeer, about 30 kilometres south of Glasgow.

Although I now had many businesses to run, I continued to make new explosives. I created a more powerful explosive called 'gelignite', beginning to sell it in 1876. Gelignite had lots of uses and it quickly became very popular. It was perfect for industries needing small explosions. You could use it to break up rock. Governments realized that it would be very useful during a war.

Business was good. We had more and more orders for dynamite, and it was difficult to make enough. I was making a lot of money, and in 1873, I bought a large house with big gardens in Paris. I employed a secretary there called Bertha Kinsky. I fell in love with Bertha, who was ten years younger than me. Unfortunately for me, she was already engaged to be married to a man called Baron Arthur von Suttner. After they married, I only met her again twice, but we often wrote to each other. She worked hard for world peace and she gave me a lot of advice in later years.

I was now making a <u>fortune</u> from sales of dynamite and gelignite around the world. I spent most of my time managing my many businesses, and life was good.

Then, one day in Paris in 1888, I had the biggest shock of my life. I picked up a newspaper and saw a headline: 'The man who sells death is dead.' I read the rest of the announcement. 'Dr Alfred Nobel,' it said, 'has died. He became rich by finding ways to kill more people faster than ever before.'

Of course, I was not dead. In fact, my older brother Ludvig had died, and the newspaper had thought it was me. But it was not the mistake that shocked me. It was not Ludvig's death that shocked me. It was those five words that shocked me. I was 'the man who sells death'. In the world's eyes, I was a killer. I was 55 years old. I asked myself many questions. What was the purpose of my life? Did I support war or peace? What should I do with my great fortune?

Those five words – 'the man who sells death' – changed my life forever. It took me seven years to decide what to do. During that time, I moved to San Remo in Italy, my final

The Nobel Prize medal

home. On 27th November 1895, at the Swedish-Norwegian Club in Paris, I announced my decision. I put 31 million Swedish kronor (today, worth about US$265 million) into a special bank account. The money was for prizes for work that helped humanity.

I chose five prizes – for Physics, Chemistry, Medicine, Literature and Peace – to be given each year. I called them the Nobel Prizes. The prize winners could be any nationality, race or religion. Each prize was a large amount of money so that the winner could continue his or her work.

Of course, the money came from dynamite, and dynamite could be used for peace or war. People could use it to help their communities, but also to kill each other. I could not change the past, however. Now I wanted to help the world to build a better future.

The first Nobel Prizes were awarded in 1901. But I did not live to see that day. I died on 10th December 1896, at my home in San Remo in Italy. I was 63 years old.

The Life of Alfred Nobel

1833   Alfred Bernhard Nobel was born in Stockholm, Sweden, the third son of Immanuel and Andriette Nobel. Alfred's father, Immanuel Nobel, lost all his money. He tried to start a new company in Finland.

1838   Immanuel moved again, this time to St Petersburg in Russia, where he set up an engineering company.

1842   When Alfred was nine, he moved with his mother Andriette and two older brothers to join his father in St Petersburg in Russia. He was taught at home with his brothers, and became interested in chemistry.

1850   Alfred spent a year in Paris, working with the French chemist Professor Jules Pelouze. He also travelled in Italy and the USA, where he saw the latest technological inventions.

1862   Alfred returned from the USA and joined the family firm in Sweden, starting to experiment with nitroglycerin.

1863   He began to sell his new explosives. The Nobel family set up a new business at Heleneborg in Sweden, where they tested new chemical mixtures.

1864 Alfred's younger brother, Emil, was killed in an explosion, together with company workers. The family continued the business, while Alfred decided to set up his own company. He called it Nitroglycerin AB.

1865 He moved to Germany and set up the Alfred Nobel & Company factory near Hamburg. An enormous explosion destroyed his factory. He made a more stable explosive, which he named 'dynamite'.

1866 He took his business to other countries, opening the United States Blasting Oil Company.

1871 He started a new business called the British Dynamite Company (later known as Nobel's Explosives Company) at Ardeer in Scotland.

1873 Alfred moved to Paris, where he bought a large house and gardens, and set up another dynamite factory.

1876 He created a more powerful explosive called 'gelignite' which sold very well.

1876 He employed Bertha Kinsky von Chinic und Tettau as a secretary. He fell in love with her, but she returned to Vienna after a short time.

1879   He discovered that Bertha was engaged to be married to a man called Baron Arthur von Suttner. Arthur and Bertha married. Alfred and Bertha wrote letters to each other all their lives, and Alfred always listened to Bertha's ideas on world peace.

1880   He joined his Swiss and Italian companies into one, and he continued to make a lot of money.

1885   He formed a group of German explosives companies.

1888   He saw a report of his own death in a Paris newspaper. It described him as 'the man who sells death'. He saw himself through the world's eyes and spent the next seven years thinking about his life.

1891   Alfred moved to San Remo, Italy.

1895   He announced his decision at the Swedish-Norwegian Club in Paris. His plan was to use most of his fortune to create five Nobel Prizes. The money still pays for the five prizes today, which are given for the best work in Physics, Chemistry, Medicine, Literature and Peace.

1896   Before the award of the first Nobel Prize, Alfred Nobel died aged 63.

1901   The first Nobel Prizes were awarded. They are still given every year to men and women for excellent work.

Andrew Carnegie

♦ ♦

1835–1919

the businessman who built libraries for poor people

**In 1901, I became the richest man in the world.
I had made my money from iron and <u>steel</u>. I did not
want to be the world's richest man when I died, however.
So I decided to give all my money away.**

◆ ◆ ◆

My story is about a poor boy who became a very rich man.
I was born on 25th November 1835 in Scotland. My parents
both came from working families who earned a living with
their hands. My mother's family were leather workers. My
father made <u>linen</u> by hand. We lived in Dunfermline, a small
Scottish town near Edinburgh, and life was not easy. My
father had to work hard to earn enough money to buy food
for us. He was angry that life was so difficult for working
people and he joined a group called the 'Chartists'. The
Chartists were working men who wanted a better future.

At that time, only rich men were able to vote or become Members of Parliament. The Chartists believed that all men should have a vote. They were also worried about safety at work. The Industrial Revolution was happening all across Europe at this time, and people were inventing bigger and better factory machines. Because the machines were new, however, they caused many accidents. The Chartists wanted factory owners to take better care of their workers. Many people in government believed that the Chartists were dangerous revolutionaries.

Our house was a noisy house. My father and my Uncle Tom were always discussing politics. Uncle Tom did not like the queen or the church. My Uncle George loved Scotland, and often performed the poems of Robert Burns, Scotland's most famous poet. I learned an important lesson from these noisy men. If you want to change things, you must have power. And to get power, you must have money.

I had to leave school when I was only 11, so my education was short. I started learning my father's trade. But some days there was no work, and the pay was terrible. Things got worse because factories were using machines to make cheap linen. Their linen was much cheaper than our linen which was made by hand.

The year 1848 was a year of revolutions in Europe. The German philosopher Karl Marx wrote *The Communist Manifesto*, and workers in many countries wanted to improve their lives. It was a year of change for our family too.

My father came home one day and said that there was no more work. He said we had no choice – we must emigrate to the USA. Two of my mother's sisters had already moved there. We sold our furniture, packed our few things and set off on a great adventure.

The journey across the Atlantic was wonderful and terrible. I was 13 and very excited. But the sea was very rough and many of the passengers were sick. We had very little space or fresh air and the journey took 50 days. But we were the lucky ones. There were often fires on ships when they crossed the Atlantic in those days, and many people died at sea. We arrived in America on 5th July, and continued by train to Pittsburgh in Pennsylvania, where my aunts lived.

My father and I found work in a clothes factory, and we lived in a small house that one of my aunts owned. I wasn't able to go to school, so I had to teach myself in the evenings. We lived near a man with a large personal library, who allowed people to borrow his books. I always remembered his kindness.

I worked all day in the factory. The pay was terrible, and I only earned $1.20 a week. Then I had some good luck. The Ohio Telegraph Company was advertising for young men to carry messages. In those days before the internet or even telephones, messages were sent by telegraph. I got the job and was very happy. Instead of spending all day in a dark and dirty factory, I could now enjoy being in the sun and fresh air. The pay was much better too. Suddenly I was earning $5 a week. I was on my way to a better life.

There was another advantage too. Taking messages to the theatre was one of my regular jobs and I was allowed to stay and watch the plays. Often they performed Shakespeare which was an amazing experience for a young boy like me.

For three years I worked at the Telegraph Company. I learned to use the telegraph machine, and soon I was sending and receiving messages. I was a quick and happy worker. Then I got a new job as secretary to Thomas A. Scott of the Pennsylvania Railroad Company. Mr Scott became like a second father to me. He helped me to make <u>investments</u> and even lent me $600 to invest in another railway company, Adams Express. When my first <u>dividend</u> for $10 arrived in the post, I was very excited. My business career had started.

But 1856 was also a very sad year in our family, because my father died.

I made more investments, taking Mr Scott's advice. I borrowed money from the bank and <u>invested</u> in railways and railway bridges.

And then the American <u>Civil War</u> started. In 1861, the North (called the 'Union') and the South (called the 'Confederacy') of America went to war over <u>slavery</u>. Mr Scott and I were sent to Washington to help the Union Army. We set up a telegraph service, and we organized the Army's transport system. I was injured when I was cutting Confederate telegraph lines.

I was given three months off work in 1862, and I decided to visit Dunfermline with my mother. I had forgotten how beautiful Scotland was and how much I loved our country.

Four years later, the North won the war and four million black <u>slaves</u> became free. Six hundred thousand soldiers were killed in the war, and it was a terrible time for the USA. But the end of the war was a fantastic opportunity for a businessman like me. During the war, I had met useful people and I had seen opportunities. Now I invested $11,000

Cutting telegraph lines

in an oil company. Within the first year, I had already made a lot of money.

New businesses and factories were appearing everywhere in America. Railways were needed to cross the huge continent. Everybody needed <u>iron</u>, and I put my money in the iron industry. By 1865, just one year after the end of the war, I was earning $50,000 a year.

Money flowed like a river into my bank, but I knew the right thing was to spend it on other people. I hadn't forgotten our poor home in Dunfermline, and I wanted to help poor working people. The government did not help poor families in those days. Men, women and children worked for many hours in a day and nobody cared if they were hungry or sick. My father had wanted to send me to school, but we all

had to work to provide food for the family. Now I could do something to help.

I had not finished making money, however. In 1872, I visited England and saw an amazing new idea. An Englishman called Henry Bessemer had invented a new way of making good quality steel for building. This was just what America needed. Three years later, I opened my own steel factory in the USA.

In 1881, I returned again to Dunfermline with my mother for a special event. We laid the first stone for a new building – the Carnegie Library. At that moment, I remembered that kind man in Pittsburgh who opened his library to strangers. Like him, I wanted to give poor families the chance to read books. I built many libraries over the years, but the Dunfermline library was the first.

My mother was not the only woman in my life. I had met a woman called Louise Whitfield. Louise was very attractive and in 1883, we became secretly engaged. We did not marry at that time, however, because we were both caring for our elderly mothers.

In 1886, my mother and brother died within a few days of each other. During the dark days that followed, Louise was with me and gave me hope. A few months later, we married. The wedding was quiet. Ten years later, we had a daughter. Having a child gave me a new purpose in life.

At the same time, business was doing well. More people needed steel. The USA needed thousands of kilometres of new railway lines. Huge amounts of steel were needed to build the country's new <u>skyscrapers</u>. I bought new companies to add to my business <u>empire</u>, including the Homestead Steel Works. In 1892, I created the Carnegie Steel Company, bringing all my businesses into one group. I spent money on <u>philanthropic</u> projects, such as Carnegie Hall in New York City, and an arts centre in Dunfermline.

As I spent more time on <u>philanthropy</u>, I gave more power to the managers in my organization. Mr Frick, for example, managed the Homestead Steel Works. Perhaps I gave him too much power. In 1892, there was a <u>strike</u> at the steel works. The strike became a battle and ten people lost their lives. It was a terrible shock. Afterwards, I always felt guilty about those events. I thought of my father's early life, when he fought against the power of the bosses. I can only imagine his words.

I visited Scotland with Louise, and she learned to love my country as much as me. In 1898, we bought a home there, called Skibo Castle, in the Scottish Highlands. The house itself was falling down, but it stood in beautiful countryside near the sea. We built a new house with Carnegie steel and beautiful yellow stone. We put in electric light, which was new in those days. Louise and I spent many happy summer months there.

In 1901, I sold the Carnegie Steel Company to the banker J.P. Morgan for an unbelievable amount of money – $480 million. 'Congratulations, Mr Carnegie,' J.P. Morgan said to me. 'You are now the richest man in the world!'

Over the next ten years, I gave away 90 per cent of my money. In Pittsburgh in 1900, I set up the Carnegie Technical School, which became the Carnegie Mellon University. I also gave money to universities in Scotland. I built the Carnegie Library in Washington and started the Carnegie Hero Fund, which paid money to brave people who needed help.

I set up two Peace Palaces in the Netherlands and America. I started the Carnegie Teachers Pension Fund and the Carnegie Corporation, an organization for education and scientific research. Altogether, I gave away $350 million, which in today's money is about $4.3 billion. I did not believe the money was mine. I was the person in charge of giving it away.

Like many people, I was shocked by the events of the First World War, which destroyed much of Europe between 1914 and 1918. Louise and I were at Skibo Castle when the war started in July 1914. We immediately packed our bags and crossed the Atlantic to the USA. I never returned to Scotland. As war continued in Europe, we decided to buy a new country home in America. We chose Shadowbrook, in a town called Lenox in Massachusetts.

War is always good for business. The country needed steel for the war industries. I still owned <u>shares</u> in my companies, and I received large dividends. I was able to spend more money on philanthropic projects, including Carnegie Mellon University in Pittsburgh, and Carnegie libraries in many towns and cities.

Although I was only 1.52 metres tall and had a strong Scottish accent, I was able to make a big success of my life in America. I achieved my goal of helping to educate the poor. I believed that a man has not lived well if he is rich when he dies. I became the richest man in the world. I had no plans to be the richest man in the world after my death.

A few months after my daughter's wedding in April 1919, I died. I was at home, at Shadowbrook.

The Life of Andrew Carnegie

1835   Andrew Carnegie was born in Dunfermline in Scotland. He had some basic education from the age of 8, but left school early to start work and earn money for the family.

1848   The Carnegie family emigrated to Pennsylvania in America, crossing the Atlantic on an old ship called the *Wiscasset*. Andrew worked in a factory making linen with his father. He hated it.

1850   Andrew got a job at a Pittsburgh telegraph company.

1853   He was offered a new job as secretary to Thomas A. Scott of the Pennsylvania Railroad Company. Mr Scott helped Andrew begin his business career.

1856   Andrew made his first big investment, in Adams Express. It was a success.

1859   He was promoted to Superintendent at the Pennsylvania Railroad Company.

1859–1861   With other partners, he bought Storey Farm Oil Creek, which became the Columbia Oil Company. He earned nearly $20,000 in one year.

1861　The American Civil War began. Andrew and Mr Scott went to Washington to organize the army telegraph and railway services for the Union army.

1862　He had three months' rest because of bad health and he returned to Dunfermline in Scotland with his mother. As they travelled through the beautiful countryside, he realized that he missed Scotland.

1865　He left the Pennsylvania Railroad Company and started to build his own business empire.

1872　In England, he met Henry Bessemer and saw his method for producing good quality steel. He decided that this was what America needed, and took the idea back to America.

1875　He opened a steel factory in the USA.

1880　He met Louise Whitfield in New York City.

1881　He visited his hometown of Dunfermline and set up a library, the first of many.

1883　He bought the Homestead Works steel company, which produced steel for America's new skyscrapers and railways.

1884–1886　He published the first of many books and newspaper articles on politics and money.

1886   This was a terrible year for Andrew, when his mother and brother died within a few days of each other. His brother Tom had a wife and nine children. Andrew fell ill too, but recovered.

1887   Andrew and Louise Whitfield married on 22nd April. They spent their honeymoon in Britain, visiting the Isle of Wight and Scotland.

1891   Carnegie Hall in New York City opened its doors. It soon became part of the city's cultural life and today is a world famous concert hall.

1892   Andrew created the Carnegie Steel Company, which included all his business interests. There was trouble at the Homestead Works steel company. Andrew was in Europe when a strike began over pay. On 6th July, the strike became a battle. Ten people died. Andrew always felt guilty about these events.

1897   On 30th March, Louise gave birth to their daughter Margaret. Andrew's mother had been called Margaret.

1898   He bought Skibo Castle in Scotland.

1899   He created the Carnegie Steel Company, which included all his business interests.

1900   The Carnegie Technical Schools were set up in Pittsburgh. Andrew described the institution as a first class technical school for the sons of steel workers. Today it is the Carnegie Mellon University.

1901   He sold his company. It was bought by J.P. Morgan for $480 million, making Andrew Carnegie the richest man in the world. He retired and concentrated on giving away his fortune.

1902–1910   Many philanthropic projects were set up, including the Carnegie Institution, the Carnegie Teachers' Pension Fund and the Carnegie Endowment for International Peace.

1911   He created the Carnegie Corporation. By now, he had given away 90 per cent of his money.

1913   The Peace Palace in The Hague, The Netherlands, opened.

1914   When Andrew heard that there was war in Europe, he and Louise were at Skibo Castle. They immediately returned to America and Andrew never went back to Scotland.

1916   He bought Shadowbrook, a large house with land in Lenox, Massachusetts, to replace Skibo.

1919   On 22nd April, his daughter Margaret was married. On 11th August, Andrew died at Shadowbrook, aged 83. By the time of his death, he had given away $350 million.

John D. Rockefeller

◆ ◆ ◆

1839–1937

the man who made millions of dollars from oil
and gave his money away

My father was called 'Devil Bill' and he lived a wild life. I lived a careful life. But he taught me one lesson: always be clever in business. I had an amazing business career, and I became very rich. And then I gave all my money away.

◆ ◆ ◆

I was born in 1839 in New York State, in the USA. I had a long and fascinating life, and I met many interesting people. My parents were the first. My father made his own medicines and travelled from town to town, selling them in bottles. Did any of his medicines work? I couldn't say. People called him 'Devil Bill', and we didn't see much of him. My mother, Eliza, had six children, and I was the second. She was very religious and gave us a <u>stable</u> home life. She taught us how to live on very little money.

My first job was on a farm selling vegetables and working with animals. When our father occasionally came home, he showed us how to succeed in business. His methods were not always honest, but he taught us to think quickly in business.

I wanted to have a better life than my parents, and I knew that I must make money. I left school and did a three-month business course at college. Then I started work as an accountant for a company called Hewitt & Tuttle. I also met my future wife, Laura Spelman, who finished top of the class in high school.

At this time, when the family was living in Cleveland, Ohio, my father did a terrible thing. He set up a secret second life in New York. He gave himself another name and married a second wife.

I enjoyed my accounting job. I was a very careful person, and I loved to write the numbers in perfect lines. But I wanted to do more than this. I dreamed of earning $100,000 a year although I was actually earning 50 cents a day at the time. I also wanted to live to be 100 years old!

My chance came in 1859, when oil was discovered in Titusville, Pennsylvania. I decided that oil was going to be very important in the modern world. A friend called Maurice B. Clark and I borrowed money and started a business together, looking for oil in Titusville. Oil was called 'black gold'. The work was hard and dirty, but it was all worth it when we found oil!

The future for our business was looking good, but trouble was coming in America. The Civil War between the North (the Union) and the South (the Confederacy) broke that same year. It was a terrible war. Six hundred thousand American soldiers died, and many thousands were injured. I was on the Union side, which wanted to stop slavery, but I

Finding oil in Titusville

did not want to fight. I gave money to the Union Army, and I continued to manage my business.

In 1863, Maurice and I bought <u>shares</u> in an oil <u>refinery</u> in Cleveland. A chemist, Samuel Andrews, had started the company. Five of us now owned it – Maurice, his two brothers, Samuel and me. But we often argued and it was hard to make good business decisions. So in 1865, I bought all the shares belonging to the three Clark brothers. We gave the company a new name – Rockefeller & Andrews – and it became the largest oil refinery in Cleveland.

At this time, I married Laura, who everyone called Cettie. We both loved the church and believed it was our duty to give to <u>charity</u>. Cettie had a good business brain too, and I often discussed big decisions with her. We were a good team. We had four daughters and a son, although sadly one of our girls died when she was very young.

After the Civil War, the country needed new railways and bridges. <u>Steam engines</u> were very important, and new industries were starting everywhere. They all needed oil. My brother, William, built another refinery in Cleveland, and we became partners. Two years later, I started a new refinery. We were beginning to make a lot of money. I moved my family to Euclid Avenue, the road where all the rich Cleveland people lived.

In 1870, I set up Standard Oil of Ohio. We invested a huge amount of money in marketing and <u>distribution</u> in order to make our oil company the biggest. We agreed prices with other oil companies, to keep them high, and bought other oil companies when we could. We bought shares in the railways, to help us control prices and distribution. By 1877, I controlled the oil industry in the USA, and I was one of the richest people in the country. In 1882, I set up the Standard Oil Trust. We had $70 million in the bank.

Standard Oil refined 90 per cent of the country's oil. People did not like this. There was no competition, they said. One newspaper described us as <u>cruel</u> and <u>greedy</u>. The government decided to change the law, to create competition in the oil business.

Industry needed more and more oil, however. We moved our head office to Broadway in New York City, a city I soon loved. The family moved too, and we built a large house. We had started to invest in iron, and now we began to sell oil abroad, to Western Europe and Asia. My father had taught me that only the strongest businessmen survive. And we were the strongest.

I did not like the negative comments, however. I had strong Christian beliefs that my mother had taught me and my wife shared. I did not make money because I wanted money. I believed in the teaching of the famous <u>preacher</u>, John Wesley, who said, 'Earn all you can, save all you can and give all you can.' I liked the <u>philanthropy</u> of Andrew Carnegie. We were <u>rivals</u> in business, but I <u>followed his example</u> in charity.

After my dear mother died in 1889, I <u>funded</u> the creation of the University of Chicago. I had always given away a tenth of the money I earned, but now it was time to give more. In 1895, I decided to retire from the business and begin a new life as a philanthropist. I was 56.

◆ ◆ ◆

Standard Oil continued to control the oil industry, with 91 per cent of production and 85 per cent of sales in 1904. I had retired from running the business, but I was president for seven more years.

In 1904, a journalist called Ida Tarbell wrote a book about the history of the company, and how it had made its money. She described all the methods I had used to defeat other oil companies. She said my business methods were unfair. The book sold thousands of copies and the publicity was bad for me and my company.

The government decided to introduce new laws about how businesses behaved. This was the beginning of the end

of Standard Oil. In 1911, the United States <u>Supreme Court</u> decided that I must divide the company into two parts.

During these difficult years, I continued to make huge amounts of money. In 1901, I set up the Rockefeller Institute of Medical Research (later called the Rockefeller University).

I gave funds to many education programmes, including the Spelman College for African-American women and millions of dollars to the University of Chicago. I wanted to pay for public health programmes too, and in 1909, the Rockefeller Sanitary Commission was set up. And, outside of the USA, I paid for a university in the Philippines.

In 1913, I set up my biggest project. It was called the Rockefeller Foundation, and it was based in New York City. It had $250 million to give to <u>programmes</u> in public health, education, art, agriculture, social science and international relations. It became the richest charity in the world.

When war broke out in Europe in 1914, I gave many millions of dollars to the government to help win the war.

Cettie and I built a country home in the Pocantico Hills outside the city. We had been married for 50 years and we celebrated our Golden Wedding anniversary there, but the following year, in 1915, my dear wife died, aged 75.

I continued to love New York City, and I built the Rockefeller Center, a huge skyscraper just off Fifth Avenue in the middle of Manhattan. This project was started in 1929, the year of the Wall Street Crash. We were able to continue building during the Depression, providing hope for the future. The project also created about 75,000 jobs for New Yorkers during those terrible years.

As part of the Rockefeller Center, we built Radio City Music Hall, a large theatre which holds an audience of 6,000. It's called the 'Showplace of the Nation', and millions of people have enjoyed concerts and shows there over the years.

'We must earn and we must give,' said John Wesley. Did I earn too much? Did I give enough? I spent the first half of my life becoming rich. I spent the second half giving my money away. I worked hard to make money and to give it away. I hope I did some good in the world.

I nearly achieved my goal of living to the age of 100. In my last years, I enjoyed the company of my children and grandchildren, and spent my time gardening and playing golf. I died of old age at 97, on 23rd May 1937.

The Life of John D. Rockefeller

1839   John Davison Rockefeller was born in
        Richford, New York, USA. He was the
        second of six children of William and Eliza
        Rockefeller.

1853   After several moves, the family arrived in
        Strongsville, Cleveland, where John went to
        high school. His future wife, Laura Spelman,
        called Cettie, was at the same school.

1855   Aged 16, he left school and did a three-
        month business course at Folsom's
        Commercial College. He then started his
        first job as an assistant accountant at Hewitt
        & Tuttle. In secret, John's father married a
        second wife and set up a second family home
        in New York City.

1859   Oil was discovered in Titusville,
        Pennsylvania, by Edwin Drake. With
        business partner, Maurice B. Clark, John
        looked for oil in Titusville, and found it.

1861   The American Civil War began. John
        supported the Union Army (the North) but
        didn't want to fight. He gave money to the
        Union Army instead.

1863   John and Maurice started an oil refinery
        business with a chemist called Samuel
        Andrews and Maurice's two brothers.

1864   John married Cettie. They later had four daughters and a son. Sadly, one of their daughters died when she was very young.

1865   He bought the Clark brothers' shares in the oil refinery, and set up Rockefeller & Andrews, which became the largest refinery in Cleveland.

1868   He made business agreements with railway companies, starting with Erie Railroad Company, in an attempt to take control of the oil business. The family moved to Euclid Avenue, Cleveland, where the city's richest families lived.

1870   Standard Oil of Ohio was set up.

1877   Standard Oil now controlled 90 per cent of America's oil.

1879   John was now one of America's Top 20 rich people (they were all men). The State of Pennsylvania said that he controlled the oil industry unfairly.

1882   The Standard Oil Trust was set up, with John as head of the organization.

1883   John moved the family to New York City, where they built a large house as their family home.

1885   Standard Oil began selling oil to Western Europe and Asia. The company moved its head office to Broadway, Manhattan.

1889   John's mother Eliza died. He gave a large amount of money to help set up the University of Chicago.

1895   He secretly retired from the day-to-day business of Standard Oil. He stayed at the company as president. He continued to earn large amounts of money. He now concentrated on his philanthropic work.

1901   The Rockefeller Institute for Medical Research was set up, and became one of the world's largest medical research centres.

1904   The journalist Ida Tarbell wrote a book about the business methods of Standard Oil. She said that John D. Rockefeller had used unfair methods. It was the beginning of the end of Standard Oil.

1906   There were two family deaths – William, John's father, and Bessie, John and Cettie's oldest daughter.

1910   John Junior (his son) left Standard Oil. He copied his father and spent his time on philanthropy.

1911 John had to divide Standard Oil in two after a decision from the Supreme Court of the USA.

1913 He set up the Rockefeller Foundation in New York City, the largest charity in the world.

1914 War broke out in Europe. The Rockefellers gave millions of dollars to the government to help win the war.

1915 Cettie died after 50 years of marriage to John. She was 75.

1919 John helped to set up Acadia National Park in the state of Maine.

1929 The Wall Street Crash happened and the Rockefellers lost a lot of money, like everyone else. The Depression – a period of high unemployment around the world – began that year.

1930 Work began on the Rockefeller Center. It took nine years to build and created 75,000 jobs for New Yorkers during a very difficult time.

1932 John and Cettie's daughter Edith died.

1937 John D. Rockefeller died in Florida, USA. He didn't quite live to 100, as he'd hoped.

Thomas Barnardo

◆ ◆ ◆

1845–1905

the man who created homes for poor children

I was planning to become a <u>preacher</u> in China. Then, in the East End of London, I met a little boy called Jim. His clothes were full of holes. His 'home' was an old, empty building full of rats. I forgot about China.

◆ ◆ ◆

I was born on 4th July 1845 in Dublin, in Ireland. I grew up there in a Christian family. Dublin was a tough city in those days, where people suffered if they were poor or sick.

After leaving school at 16, I started to work for someone who sold wine. The next year, in 1862, I joined a religious group called the Plymouth Brethren. They taught me that alcohol was <u>evil</u> and that we should never drink it. I left the wine-seller and found a new direction for my life. I decided to become a doctor and help people. I went to London to study medicine.

In London, I joined a church and met a preacher called Hudson Taylor. He convinced me that I should go to a non-Christian country to <u>preach</u> the Bible. He said I should finish my medical studies and then go to China. In fact, I never left London.

I started medical school. There was a great deal to learn in the classroom. There was even more to learn on the streets outside. In the evenings, I went out into the East End of the city, where many of London's poor people lived and worked.

London had become a successful city because of its position on the River Thames, from where it <u>traded</u> with the rest of the world. The shipping companies employed thousands of people, who lived in terrible houses in areas like Limehouse and Wandsworth near the river. There was a lot of crime there, partly because people drank a lot of cheap alcohol. I wanted to warn them that alcohol was evil. I went into <u>pubs</u>, but often the owners threw me out. One man was particularly violent and broke two of my bones.

In 1866, many people in the East End become infected with cholera, a terrible disease which is caused by dirty drinking water. Thousands of people died and many children became <u>orphans</u>.

I decided to set up an evening school for some of these children. I found an old building in Limehouse, in London's East End. Animals had once been kept in it. Other members of my church helped to change the building into a school, and it opened in 1867. We called it the Ragged School.

After one class, a little boy didn't want to go home. His name was Jim Jarvis. He said he was ten years old, but he looked half that age. He was very thin and looked sick. His parents were dead, he told me, and he didn't have a home. I knew it wasn't enough to give him a few <u>pence</u> to buy some bread.

Although it was nearly midnight and the dark streets were dangerous, I asked him to show me where he slept. We went to an old, empty building. It was falling down, with holes in the roof. Rats ran into the corners as we went inside. A group of young boys, none of them older than fourteen, appeared from the shadows. Jim warned them not to rob me.

Like Jim, all these boys were <u>homeless</u> and <u>destitute</u>. I knew then that I didn't want to go to China. These boys needed me.

Charles Dickens, London's most famous writer, brilliantly describes these terrible conditions. His books show a society that has forgotten its poor orphan children. He created the orphan Oliver Twist, who has to live among the street children.

Some wealthier people blamed the street children for being destitute. They said the children were lazy. Sometimes the police arrested them and the courts punished them. But that was never the answer. They needed to go to school. If they could learn to read and write, and do simple maths, they could get jobs. They could learn to be proud of themselves, and be useful to society.

It was clear that the Ragged School wasn't enough. These children needed somewhere to sleep, to eat, to wash and to grow up. They needed a home among people who cared for them.

I was 25 years old and full of energy and enthusiasm. I didn't have much experience, though. A good friend, Robert Barclay, a banker, helped me to raise the money and plan the work. In 1870, we set up the Stepney Boys' Home for teenage boys. This was the first Dr Barnardo's Home. It wasn't very comfortable, but it gave the boys a bed and a roof over their heads. I also arranged jobs for them. I wanted to give them a chance to earn money and live a good life.

It wasn't long before the street children heard about the Stepney Home, and soon too many boys wanted to live in the Home. We opened a second Home in Salmon Lane, also in Stepney, and we employed two teachers and 24 staff.

Still we didn't have enough beds. One boy called John Somers arrived one night. Everyone called him 'Carrots' because he had red hair. The Home was full and he was turned away. Two days later, a policeman found him dead in the street. That same day, I ordered new signs for the front door of each Home. "No Destitute Child Ever Refused Entry", they said.

People began to give money to our Homes, and we were able to buy a large pub. We made plans for it to become a church, coffee house and home for street boys. A team of builders and helpers worked on the project, many of them sleeping in a huge tent next to the pub. There were plenty of problems, but soon it was ready to open.

I also fell in love at this time. I met Syrie Elmslie, who shared my religious and philanthropic interests, and believed in my work. We married in 1873. We were given a house called Mossford Lodge as a wedding present, which became a home for poor girls. At first there were beds for only 12 girls, but soon 60 girls lived there. In 1876, we created the Girls' Village Home. This was a collection of cottages around a village green, with room for 1,500 girls. We taught them how to clean a house, work in a shop or be a nurse, so they could go into jobs when they left the Home.

To get more publicity, I wrote a book about the Barnardo's story so far, called *How It All Happened*. I had another fund-raising idea, but this one was less successful. I set up a photography studio at our first Stepney Boys' Home. We took a photograph of each new boy on the day he arrived. We took a second photo of the boy after a few months with us, when he looked healthy and happy. These 'Before' and 'After' pictures showed very clearly the work that our Homes did. We sold the photos to raise money, and they were very successful.

But some people didn't believe that the photographs were real. I was also accused of other crimes. Some parents said I had stolen their children. Other people said that we did not look after the children properly and that we stole money from the Homes. I appeared in court several times, but I was never found guilty of any <u>charge</u>. I stopped selling the photos, however.

I continued with my medical studies, but of course I couldn't give them my full attention. Most of my time was spent running the Children's Homes. I decided to set up a committee to help me, and businessmen and church ministers agreed to join it. This gave me more time to improve the children's health.

By 1878, we had opened more than 50 Homes for orphans in the London area. But we never had enough money. The government supported us with words but not with money. The big churches too were slow to offer help. We had to come up with new ideas.

One idea was the <u>emigration</u> programme. We sent groups of Barnardo's boys across the Atlantic Ocean. They left the dangerous and dirty streets of London's East End and arrived in the fresh air and open spaces of Canada. I hoped this would give them an opportunity for a better life. It became clear many years later that some of the boys were <u>treated</u> badly, however. They had to work long hours and sleep in old farm buildings. Others found their new lives better than the streets of London.

In London, we set up a home for children with <u>mental problems</u>. One of our own daughters suffered in this way, and Syrie and I wanted to help other families in the same situation. Also, in those days, if a young woman had a baby before she was married, she was not allowed to keep it. We helped to find homes for these babies. We also arranged work nearby for the young mother so she could spend time with her child on her days off.

In 1891, we had another new idea. We set up the Young Helpers' League, a fund-raising organization. We taught music in all our Barnardo's Homes. I invited the best musicians to join a band, which we called the Musical Boys. I sent them to Australia and New Zealand to play concerts in order to raise money. They did well, receiving enough funds to set up the Australasian Hospital in England, at the Girls' Village.

I was active in politics too. In 1891, I worked hard with my friends in Parliament to create a new law. It said that a child's needs were more important than the rights of the parents. In other words, parents didn't own their children.

Although I was only in my fifties, I was feeling tired. I had problems with my heart so I had to do less work. One of my last projects was a school in Norfolk, which trained 300 street boys for a life at sea in the Navy. A few years later, in 1905, I died. At that time, we were running 96 Barnardo's Homes, and caring for 8,500 children, giving them hope for the future.

The Life of Thomas Barnardo

1845   Thomas John Barnardo was born in Dublin, Ireland. His family was very religious, and he hated to see poor and hungry people on the city streets.

1861   When he was 16, he left school and began working for a wine-seller.

1862   He joined a church group called the Plymouth Brethren. They believed that alcohol was evil, and Thomas decided he was in the wrong business.

1866   Thomas moved to London. He wanted to study medicine and become a doctor. He met a preacher called Hudson Taylor. Taylor convinced him that he should go to a non-Christian country to preach the Bible.

1866   In London a disease called cholera killed more than 3,000 people, so there were many orphans.

1867   The Ragged School opened in Limehouse, a school for poor boys in London's East End. A young boy called Jim Jarvis came to his school. Jim showed Thomas the reality of life for London's street children, who had no food, no home and no hope. Thomas forgot about China and decided to spend his life helping poor orphans.

1870   A friend, Robert Barclay, who was a
        banker, and Lord Shaftesbury, a Member
        of Parliament, gave Thomas money. He
        opened the Stepney Boys' Home in the East
        End of London. This was the first of the Dr
        Barnardo's Homes.

1872   With money from friends, Thomas bought
        a large pub called the Edinburgh Castle in
        Limehouse. A team of helpers and builders
        turned it into a church, coffee house and
        home for street children. To raise more
        money, he wrote and published a book
        about the Barnardo's story so far called
        How it All Happened.

1873   He had met Syrie Elmslie through
        his work. She shared his religious and
        philanthropic interests, and they soon
        married. They were given a house called
        Mossford Lodge in Barkingside, Essex, near
        London, as a wedding present. They turned
        it into a home for orphan girls.

1875   He set up a committee to run the homes.
        He became the Director of Homes. He
        started a magazine called *The Night and Day
        Magazine* to tell people about the work of
        Barnardo's.

1876   Thomas finally took his medical exams. He never became a fully qualified doctor, but he received a qualification from the Royal College of Surgeons. This allowed him to work as a doctor. Mossford Lodge was now too small. The Girls' Village Home was set up, also in Barkingside.

1877   Thomas was accused of treating some of the children badly, stealing money from Barnardo's and taking children from their parents. He was found not guilty. He received new gifts of money for his work because of all the publicity.

1878   The fiftieth Dr Barnardo's Home opened in London.

1879   A dangerous disease called scarlet fever broke out at the Girls' Village Home in Barkingside. None of the girls died, showing that the Home was caring for the girls properly.

1881   Thomas started his emigration programme. The first group of 51 boys went to Canada, with a second group sent to Australia soon after. It later became known that many of these boys were badly treated.

1887   Thomas had another idea and sent street boys out of London to homes outside of the city.

1889   He arranged for families to take in the babies of girls who were not married. He found work for the girls near to the babies' homes, so that the mothers and their children could spend a little time together.

1891   The Musical Boys travelled to Australia and New Zealand to raise money for Barnardo's with concerts.

1901   The Watts Naval Training School was set up in Norfolk.

1905   Thomas died in London, aged 60. Barnardo's was running 96 homes and caring for 8,500 street children on the day he died. His work continues today, run by the Barnardo's <u>charity</u>.

Henry Wellcome

• ◆ •

1853–1936

the man who used his money for medical research

I was born in the American <u>Wild West</u>. I was attacked by Sioux Indians, my college was destroyed by fire and I searched for rare plants in Ecuador's rainforest. I became a businessman and a collector. I even shook hands with the King of England.

◆ ◆ ◆

I was born in 1853 in the American Wild West. My parents lived in a <u>log cabin</u> in Almond, a small village in Wisconsin where the winters were very long and cold. My father was a <u>preacher</u>. In the warmer months, we travelled from village to village, living in a <u>covered wagon</u>. Father stood on a box and preached in every place we came to. He warned people about the dangers of drinking alcohol. Life was hard in the villages and small towns that we visited. People were very poor, and often had no medicine when they were ill. I thought someone should bring medicines to these people.

In Almond, life was hard for us too. The roads were only rough tracks. My father was a farmer as well as a preacher, earning just enough from growing potatoes to feed the family. I worked in the potato fields when I was old enough. We were <u>white settlers</u> living in Native American Indian lands. I learnt how to survive by watching the Native Americans.

In 1861, we needed all our skills when the potato crop failed. It was a terrible time. We had no money and no food, and we had to leave Almond. We put our few things in the covered wagon and set off to Garden City, Minnesota, where my uncle lived. The road was rough and the 500-kilometre journey was long. It was dangerous too. We travelled through Native Indian territory, expecting an attack at any moment. Travellers were often killed. We were lucky, however, and arrived safely in Garden City several weeks later.

My brother and I went to school at the local log-cabin school. We learnt how to ride and hunt. It was a good life. Then in 1862, during the American <u>Civil War</u>, a small war started between the Sioux Indians and the white settlers in Minnesota. The Sioux were very unhappy because the white American government owed them money for their land, but refused to pay it.

After a terrible year when the crops failed, the Sioux were hungry and desperate. Their <u>chief</u>, Little Crow, led them to war. They rode into Garden City and other Minnesota towns on horses. We were very frightened, and thought they were going to kill us. The children's job was to help look after the injured people. After many people were killed on

both sides, the settlers won the war. In December of 1862, 38 Sioux Indian chiefs were <u>hanged</u>. I never forgot this war, and I decided I would work for peace during my life.

My uncle had a pharmacy, and when I was 13, I started work there. My job was to mix the medicines for his customers. I became fascinated by chemistry, and my uncle allowed me to experiment with new recipes. I went with him on his visits to patients, and learnt some medical skills. I learnt how to <u>treat</u> cuts and mend broken bones.

I had a natural talent for business as well as chemistry. In 1869, when I was 16, I invented "Wellcome's Invisible Ink" and advertised it in the local newspaper. The idea of invisible ink is that it disappears when it dries, so that you can send secret messages. When you receive a secret message, you heat it, and the words appear again. I'd actually made the 'ink' from lemon juice. I discovered that I was good at selling things and I made some money.

When I wanted to start work, I moved to Rochester, a city about 160 kilometres from Garden City. I went to see Dr William Worrall Mayo there, a doctor who was a friend of my uncle's. He had an interesting human skeleton in his office. It was the skeleton of an Indian chief who was hanged in 1862. Dr Mayo helped me to get a job in a pharmacy and taught me chemistry and physics. My success in life is because of Dr Mayo, who encouraged me to go to college in Chicago and train as a pharmacist.

I was a student in Chicago in 1871 when a huge fire started in the city. There were strong winds that day, and the fire burnt through the city. The heat was unbelievable as the fire destroyed many of the city's wooden buildings. Three hundred people died and 100,000 of them lost their homes. My college was burnt to the ground, and all the students had to leave. I moved to Philadelphia, where I worked for a pharmacist by day and went to classes at the College of Pharmacy in the evening. I learnt a lot about making and selling drugs.

I made friends with another student called Silas Burroughs. He came from a wealthy family, and was very friendly and charming. His personality made him a great salesman.

After college, I moved to New York City, where I became a medical salesman. I worked hard and was successful at selling, and in 1878 my manager asked me to join an expedition to Ecuador in South America. The goal was to find the cinchona tree so we could make quinine.

Quinine is used to treat malaria, a disease that is common in hot countries and kills about a million people a year around the world. Malaria is caused by mosquito bites. My company wanted to make a treatment for malaria from quinine. I was 25 and ready for an adventure.

In June 1878, we sailed to the coast of Ecuador, and travelled into the countryside. We bought donkeys, and local Indians took us along the dangerous mountain paths. We saw human bones lying among the rocks below, and we knew that many visitors never returned from their journeys. The bones were white because the sun had baked them. We followed our guides into the dark rainforest, until finally we found cinchona trees. We cut many of the trees down and loaded the men and donkeys with them.

Our return journey through the mountains was even harder, travelling slowly along the narrow paths with our heavy loads. Although I was pleased at our success, I was not happy about cutting down the trees. It was bad for the natural environment.

I wrote to Silas and told him about my trip to Ecuador. His reply took a long time to arrive, and as I read his letter, I understood why. He had moved to London, where he had set up his own pharmaceutical company. He was selling medicine which had been made into tablets. This was a completely new idea. Medicines were usually sold as liquids in bottles or as powders in packets. Sales were very good. He asked me to join him in London, and I made the long journey across the Atlantic from the USA.

Silas showed me around London. He took me to his factory and we discussed his business long into the night. We decided that two Americans could definitely run a good business in London. We shook hands, and in 1880 we set up Burroughs Wellcome & Company.

We worked day and night to start the business. We spent a lot on advertisements. Sales grew. Silas travelled the world, finding new places to sell our tablets. By the time I was celebrating my thirtieth birthday, four years later, we were rich men. We opened offices in other countries – in China, the USA, India, Canada and Italy. We started to sell other medical supplies, as well as tablets. Our company became famous, and we had kings and presidents among our customers.

Like me, Silas was very religious. He also had very <u>liberal</u> political views, and Burroughs Wellcome & Company was very liberal to its workers. We introduced an eight-hour working day and gave <u>shares</u> to our workers. Our factory had attractive gardens for people to use at lunchtime, and we organized sports and social events for them.

As the company became richer, we were able to pay for new research. Because we were a business rather than a research institute, however, some scientists refused to work for us. People said that science and business did not mix. So in 1894, I set up the Wellcome Research Laboratories, a <u>philanthropic</u> organization.

Silas and I began to argue, however. I was more interested in making money than him, and I wanted to make Burroughs Wellcome & Company bigger. Perhaps because he came from a rich family, money was less important to him than to me. By the early 1890s, we had stopped speaking to each other and we decided to divide the company into two smaller companies. While our lawyers were working on that, however, Silas died suddenly in 1895. He was only 48.

I travelled widely in Africa to find out more about malaria, a subject of special interest to me. While I was in Khartoum in the Sudan in 1901, I met a girl called Syrie Barnardo. She was very interested in my work and I fell in love with her. She was the daughter of Thomas Barnardo. We came back to London together and got married the same year. We had a son, Henry Mounteney, in 1903.

I continued to travel and returned to Africa, wanting to find out more about malaria. My trip to Ecuador had started my interest in the disease. We did an experiment in Khartoum, in the Sudan, an area where malaria was common. We removed the water from the place where the mosquitoes lived. The number of deaths from malaria fell by 90 per cent.

A great discovery was made in Uganda in 1903 by the British scientist, Dr David Bruce. He was researching 'sleeping sickness', and he found that the tsetse fly carried the infection. In order to fight this terrible disease, I set up the Wellcome Medical Hospital Dispensary in Kampala, the capital of Uganda.

My marriage to Syrie was not a success. I was away for long periods of time on business and in 1909, we agreed to live separate lives. At the same time, I decided to become a British citizen and in 1910, I was very proud to receive my British passport.

I was always fascinated by archaeology as well as medical matters. Between 1911 and 1914 I organized a dig in Sudan, at an ancient town called Jebel Moya, about 240 kilometres south of Khartoum. I worked there with 3,000 local people, looking for pieces of ancient pots, tools and jewellery. I loved collecting, and wanted to build up important collections to give to the world. One of my collections went on display in 1913, in the Wellcome Historical Medical Museum in London. It was my huge collection of medical objects, which included Napoleon's toothbrush!

After 1914, my business grew faster than ever, but for the wrong reasons. There was war in Europe, and huge quantities of medicines were needed to treat injured soldiers. Millions of men were killed and injured in the battles.

The following 12 months was a sad time for me, as my marriage to Syrie came to an end legally. The judge decided that our son, Henry, must live with me. To forget about my personal problems, I worked harder than ever. My business took all my time.

New medicines were being developed, and it was time to expand the business again. I invested a lot of money in medical research. I continued to add to my collection of medical equipment because I wanted to keep our history for the future.

In 1924, I set up the Wellcome Foundation Limited, which brought all my interests together. It included the pharmaceutical company which made the money, the medical research sections, the museums and their collections. In 1931, I decided to start building a new home for my research laboratories, and my collections. It was called the Wellcome Research Institution and opened a year later.

The next year, I became Sir Henry Wellcome and I met the King. The small boy who had lived in a covered wagon was now shaking hands with King George V of England. I was very proud. I died in 1936 in London, the home of the Wellcome Foundation.

The Life of Henry Wellcome

1853   Henry Solomon Wellcome was born on
        21st August in a log cabin in Almond,
        Wisconsin, USA. His father was a travelling
        preacher and potato farmer. It was a very
        strict religious household.

1861   The potato crop failed and the Wellcome
        family moved to Garden City, Minnesota.
        Henry's uncle lived there, and Henry and
        his brother went to a local log-cabin school.

1862   The Sioux Indians attacked Garden City.
        Many adults were injured, and Henry
        helped to look after them.

1866   He left school and went to work for his
        uncle, who was a chemist.

1869   He invented "Invisible Ink" and advertised
        it in the local newspaper. It was actually
        lemon juice.

1870   He left home and went to the city of
        Rochester, Minnesota, where he worked for
        Dr William Worrall Mayo, a friend of his
        uncle. Dr Mayo taught Henry chemistry and
        physics and encouraged him to take a college
        course in <u>pharmaceuticals</u>.

1871   After his college was destroyed in the Great
       Chicago Fire of 1871, Henry moved to
       Philadelphia to continue his studies. At
       the College of Pharmacy there, he met his
       future business partner, Silas Burroughs.

1874   He graduated from college and moved
       to New York City, where he became a
       travelling salesman.

1878   His company sent him on an adventure to
       Ecuador. The goal was to find the cinchona
       tree so they could make quinine.

1880   Henry moved to London to join his friend
       Silas Burroughs in his new business. Until
       then, medicines were sold as powders
       or liquids. Silas was selling medicines
       as tablets. The new business was called
       Burroughs Wellcome & Company.

1883   The company did well and they bought
       their first factory in Wandsworth in south
       London.

1894   Henry started the Wellcome Physiological
       Research Laboratories.

1895   Silas died, aged 48, leaving Henry in
       charge of the company.

1901   Henry met a young woman called Syrie Barnardo in Khartoum. They returned to London and married soon after.

1902   He set up the Wellcome Tropical Research Laboratories in Khartoum.

1903   Syrie gave birth to their son, Henry Mounteney. A new treatment for sleeping sickness was discovered in Africa, and Henry set up the Wellcome Medical Hospital Dispensary in Kampala in Uganda.

1910   Henry received a British passport. He travelled to Panama, to help the United States government deal with malaria among the building workers on the Panama Canal project.

1911–1914   He set up a dig at the ancient town of Jebel Moya in the Sudan.

1913   He opened the Wellcome Historical Medical Museum in London to display his collection of medical objects.

1914   The First World War broke out.

1916   Henry and Syrie's marriage ended, and their son Henry went to live with his father.

1918   The Wellcome Foundation Limited was set up. All Henry's interests were now in one organization.

1932   The Wellcome Research Institution opened. It housed the Wellcome research laboratories and Henry's huge collection of books and medical objects. Henry became Sir Henry Wellcome and met King George V of the United Kingdom. He became a Fellow of the Royal Society and a Fellow of the Royal College of Surgeons.

1936   Henry died on 25th July in London. He was 82.

Madam C. J. Walker

• ◆ •

1867–1919

the woman who gave her money to the
African-American community

My parents were <u>slaves</u> but I was not. I picked cotton, cleaned houses and washed clothes until I was nearly forty. Then I created a great hair product, and in just thirteen years, I became the richest black woman in the United States of America!

♦ ◆ ♦

I was born Sarah Breedlove in 1867 into a family of people who had been slaves, but I was not a slave. Two years before my birth, the American <u>Civil War</u> ended and <u>slavery</u> became against the law. Four million slaves were freed on 6th December 1865. Although life did not become easy for African-American people, at least I was a free person from the beginning of my life.

In my early years, I lived on a large farm in Delta, Louisiana. We were very poor and if we fell ill, there were no medicines for us. By the time I was seven, both my parents had died. It was a very sad time, and my brothers and sister and I felt very angry too. White people had medicines, so why were there no medicines to <u>treat</u> our parents?

I had one sister and four brothers, and now we were <u>orphans</u>. My sister Louvenia and I worked in the cotton fields, earning very little money. The work was terrible, especially for children. When I was ten, Louvenia and I moved to Vicksburg in Mississippi. We worked long hours cleaning houses there, with no time for school.

Life was not good at home either, as Louvenia's husband Willie Powell <u>treated</u> me very badly. I was only 14 but I needed to escape from his house. So in 1881, I married Moses McWilliams, and three years later, I had a daughter. We called her A'Lelia. I was only 17 but I was enjoying being a mother.

Our happy family life lasted only two years. Moses died, and I was very sad. I had a child to look after, however, and I had to plan her future. We made the long journey north to St Louis, Missouri, where my four brothers lived and worked. They helped me find a place to live and a job washing clothes. I didn't earn much money, but I saved enough to pay for A'Lelia to go to school.

In 1894, I met and married my second husband, John Davis. I joined a new church, and I made good friends among the African-American women there. They introduced me to the world of politics, and I realized that African-American people needed to fight for their rights. I joined a <u>civil rights</u> organization called the National Association of Colored Women. This was a long time before the Civil Rights <u>movement</u> of Dr Martin Luther King. Black people had to wait until the 1960s before they won the right to vote.

My marriage to John was not going well, and I was very unhappy when it ended in 1903. My hair started to fall out, partly because of the stress. I was embarrassed by my appearance, and I didn't want to go out of the house. I tried different <u>products</u> to make my hair grow back, including one made by Annie Malone. It actually worked! I was very pleased with the results, and in 1905, I moved to Denver, Colorado, to become a salesperson for Annie Malone products. My time with Annie Malone taught me a lot about how to run a business.

I met my third husband in Denver. Charles J. Walker worked in the newspaper business, and we married in 1906. At about the same time, I started experimenting with my own hair <u>treatments</u>. I created Madam Walker's Wonderful Hair Grower. Everyone started to call me Madam Walker, a name

Madam Walker's hair product

I liked! I found that I was good at selling, and my product became popular. With Charles encouraging me, I developed more products. I decided to start my own business, which was unusual for an African-American woman in those days.

That decision changed my life. Charles and I spent 18 months travelling around the USA, selling my hair products. All over the south of the country, we met black people who had come from slave families like me. They wanted to look good and improve their chances in life.

I loved selling and communicating with my customers. I showed and sold my products in shops, markets and churches, and I went to people's houses to sell them. We also advertised in national newspapers. At home in Denver, my daughter A'Lelia sent out products that people ordered by post.

Just two years later, in 1908, I was able to open a school for hairdressers in Pittsburgh. I called it Lelia College, using my daughter's name. Hair care was becoming an important business in America, and I began to make a lot of money. In 1910, I set up a factory in Indianapolis, with a training college for my salespeople. I also gave money to a building project. The project was to create a home for young African-American people. This was my first big philanthropic gift, and I wanted to do more philanthropy.

My third marriage came to an end in 1912, perhaps because the business and travelling took so much of my time. I was 45 and I needed a change, so from 1913 to 1916 I travelled around Central America and the Caribbean. In 1916, I moved to New York City. My daughter and I built a new house and business in Harlem, and we called it the Walker Salon. We built a factory too.

The First World War had started in Europe in 1914. Many American soldiers lost their lives or came home injured, including many African-Americans. When black soldiers returned to Harlem, it was important to treat them well, I believed. I supported projects to help them get back to normal life. Many people lived in dirty, dangerous houses and ate a bad diet in Harlem. Many were out of work. I hated to see their difficult lives. I spent less time on my business so that I could become more active in politics.

A terrible battle between blacks and whites took place in East St Louis in 1917. The <u>steel</u> factories needed workers because so many men had gone to the war in Europe. Thousands of black workers arrived from the southern states. White workers were afraid of losing their jobs, and there was <u>tension</u> between whites and blacks in the hot July weather.

The tension increased, and there were battles in the streets. Many black people were killed. Thousands more people lost their homes in fires around East St Louis. The city law officers did very little to protect innocent people. Several black men were 'lynched', meaning they were <u>hanged</u>, without a trial.

I joined the National Association for the Advancement of Colored People (NAACP). About 10,000 black people <u>marched</u> through New York City to show their feelings about the events in East St Louis, and I went with them. I also gave money to help the NAACP. During that year, I visited Woodrow Wilson, the President of the USA. He agreed to see me because of my business success. I tried to persuade President Wilson to make lynching a serious crime. Black people needed more protection from law officers, I told him.

As well as fighting for changes in the law, I believed in giving African-American people opportunities. I had become powerful because I was rich and successful. I organized a national conference in Philadelphia for hairdressers from all over the country. It was a great event! Many businesswomen came and showed ordinary women how to be successful. We talked about how business and politics could change the lives of black women.

I moved to a new home in 1918 in New York City. It was called Villa Lewaro, and I loved living there and inviting guests to visit me. It was designed by Vertner Tandy, New York's first African-American architect. I was really enjoying life, and feeling that I was helping a few people in the world. Then I got some bad news. Although I was only 51, I had a serious illness.

I wanted my business and <u>social programmes</u> to continue. I had become successful, and I hoped other people could <u>follow my example</u>. The secrets of my success were hard work, confidence, good quality products and honesty in business. But the most important thing was hard work.

My daughter A'Lelia became president of the Madam C.J. Walker Manufacturing Company. I believed I had been a good example to her. I had become the first black businesswoman to make a million dollars and I was the richest African-American woman in the United States of America. That was a big achievement for a girl from the cotton fields of Louisiana!

But the important thing is what you do with your money. I <u>left</u> two-thirds of my money to charities, schools, homes for orphans and old people, especially in the African-American community. I died when I was only 51 but I believe I was able to do some good.

The Life of Madam C. J. Walker

1867 Her name was Sarah Breedlove when she was born in Delta, Louisiana, and she was one of six children. She was born free, two years after the end of slavery.

1872 Her mother died.

1874 Her father died of yellow fever and she lived with her older sister, Louvenia.

1877 Louvenia and her husband moved to Vicksburg, Mississippi, taking the orphan Sarah with them. They cleaned houses.

1881 Sarah married Moses McWilliams, to escape from her sister's husband, who treated her badly.

1885 She gave birth to a daughter, A'Lelia.

1887 After her husband Moses died, she took her daughter to St Louis, where her four brothers worked. She found work washing clothes to pay for her daughter to go to school.

1894 She got married again, this time to John Davis. She continued to do washing and cleaning, and started going to night school to learn to read and write. She joined St Paul's African Methodist Episcopal Church.

1903   She separated from her husband. She began to experience hair loss, and tried the hair products made by African–American businesswoman, Annie Malone. The products worked!

1905   She moved to Denver, Colorado, and started working for Annie Malone's company.

1906   Sarah got married again, this time to Charles Joseph Walker, who worked in the newspaper business. She began experimenting with her own hair treatments, including one that she called Madam Walker's Wonderful Hair Grower. She became known as Madam Walker and began to travel around the USA, selling and advertising her products.

1908   She moved with her family to Pittsburgh, where she opened a school for hairdressers called Lelia College.

1910   She set up a factory in Indianapolis to make her products. She also set up a training college for her salespeople.

1911   The business was a big success and she employed thousands of people. She became a millionaire.

1912   Her marriage to Charles ended.

1913–1916   Madam Walker travelled around Central America and the Caribbean.

1916   She moved to New York City and became a philanthropist and joined many organizations, including the National Association for the Advancement of Colored People (NAACP). She gave money to many educational programmes. She bought a house and opened a beauty shop next door, called the Walker Salon.

1917   Madam Walker asked the President of the USA to change the law on lynching – hanging a person, usually a black person, without a trial. She arranged a national conference in Philadelphia, for black women in the hairdressing business.

1918   She moved to Villa Lewaro, a large house and garden in New York City. The house was designed by Vertner Tandy, the first African-American architect in New York.

1919   She died at Villa Lewaro, aged 51. She was the first black female American millionaire and the richest African-American woman in America. A'Lelia replaced her mother as president of the Madam C.J. Walker Manufacturing Company.

archaeology UNCOUNTABLE NOUN
Archaeology is the study of the past by examining the remains of things such as buildings and tools.

charge COUNTABLE NOUN
A **charge** is a formal accusation that someone has committed a crime.

charity COUNTABLE NOUN
A **charity** is an organization which raises money to help people who are ill, disabled, or poor.
UNCOUNTABLE NOUN
Charity is behaviour that shows kindness and generosity to people who are less fortunate than you.

chief COUNTABLE NOUN
A **chief** is the leader of a group of American Indians.

civil rights PLURAL NOUN
Civil rights are the rights that people have to equal treatment and equal opportunities, whatever their race, sex, or religion.

civil war NOUN
A **civil war** is a war that is fought between different groups of people living in the same country.

cliff COUNTABLE NOUN
A **cliff** is a high area of land with a very steep side, especially one next to the sea.

covered wagon COUNTABLE NOUN
A **covered wagon** is a wagon that has a curved canvas roof and is pulled by horses. Covered wagons were used by the Europeans as they travelled west across the United States.

cruel ADJECTIVE
Someone who is **cruel** deliberately causes pain or unhappiness and does not have any sympathy for weaker people.

Depression PROPER NOUN
The Depression was a period of about 10 years starting in 1929 when a lot of companies stopped working and a lot of people lost their jobs.

destitute ADJECTIVE
Someone who is **destitute** has no money or possessions.

devil COUNTABLE NOUN
You can use **devil** when showing how you feel about someone. For example, you can call someone 'a devil' if you think they live a wild and uncontrolled sort of life.

dig COUNTABLE NOUN
A **dig** is an organized activity in which people dig into the ground in order to discover ancient historical objects.

distribution UNCOUNTABLE NOUN
Distribution is the sending of goods from one place to a lot of different other places.

dividend COUNTABLE NOUN
A **dividend** is the part of a company's profits which is paid to people who have shares in the company.

emigrate INTRANSITIVE VERB
If you **emigrate**, you leave your own country to go and live in another.

emigration UNCOUNTABLE NOUN
Emigration is when people leave their own country to go and live in another country.

empire COUNTABLE NOUN
A business **empire** is a group of companies controlled by one powerful person.

evil ADJECTIVE
If you describe something as **evil**, you mean that it is morally bad and causes harm to people.

example
to follow sb's example PHRASE
If you **follow** someone's **example**, you copy their behaviour, especially because you admire them.

explosive VARIABLE NOUN
An **explosive** is a substance that can cause an explosion.
ADJECTIVE
An **explosive** substance or device is one that can cause an explosion.

fortune COUNTABLE NOUN
A **fortune** is a very large amount of money. If you **make a fortune** from a particular activity, you earn a lot of money by doing it.

fund TRANSITIVE VERB
To **fund** something means to provide the money it needs so that it can start or continue to happen.

fund-raising UNCOUNTABLE NOUN
Fund-raising is the activity of collecting money for a particular purpose.

greedy ADJECTIVE
Someone who is **greedy** wants more of something than is necessary or fair.

hang (hangs, hanging or **hanged)** TRANSITIVE VERB
If someone **is hanged**, they are killed by having a rope tied around their neck and the support taken away from under their feet.

homeless ADJECTIVE
You describe people who have nowhere to live as **homeless**.

humanity UNCOUNTABLE NOUN
All the people in the world can be referred to as **humanity**.

Industrial Revolution
PROPER NOUN
The Industrial Revolution was the process that happened in the nineteenth century when countries began developing industry and people moved into cities away from the countryside.

invest TRANSITIVE VERB,
INTRANSITIVE VERB
If you **invest in** something, or if you **invest** a sum of money, you use your money in a way that you hope will increase its value, for example by buying shares or property.

investment COUNTABLE NOUN
An **investment** is an amount of money that you invest, or the thing that you invest it in.

iron UNCOUNTABLE NOUN
Iron is a dark grey metal. It is made from iron ore, which comes out of the ground.

leave (leaves, leaving or **left)**
TRANSITIVE VERB
If you **leave** property or money **to** someone, you arrange for it to be given to them after you have died.

liberal ADJECTIVE
If someone has **liberal views**, or if they are **liberal**, they are tolerant and believe in people's right to behave differently or hold their own opinions.

linen UNCOUNTABLE NOUN
Linen is a kind of cloth that is made from a plant called flax.

literature UNCOUNTABLE NOUN
Novels, plays, and poetry are referred to as **literature**, especially when they are considered to be very artistic.

log cabin COUNTABLE NOUN
A **log** cabin is a simple house made from wood. **Log cabins** were often built by the people who lived in them.

march INTRANSITIVE VERB
When a large group of people **march**, they walk somewhere together in order to protest about something.

Member of Parliament
COUNTABLE NOUN
A **Member of Parliament** is a person who has been elected to represent people in a country's parliament. It is usually abbreviated to **MP**.

mental problem NOUN
If someone has **mental problems**, their mind is not in a healthy state, which causes them to behave in an unusual or difficult way.

movement COUNTABLE NOUN
A **movement** is a group of people who share the same beliefs, ideas, and aims and who work to make changes that will achieve those aims.

orphan COUNTABLE NOUN
An **orphan** is a child whose parents are dead.

pence PLURAL NOUN
Pence is the plural of **penny**, which is the smallest unit of money in Britain. There are 100 **pence** in a pound. Before 1971, there were 240 **pence** in a pound.

pharmaceutical ADJECTIVE
Pharmaceutical means connected with the industrial production of medicines.
PLURAL NOUN
Pharmaceuticals are medicines.

philanthropic ADJECTIVE
A **philanthropic** person or organization gives money or other help to people who need it, even though they do not have to.

philanthropy UNCOUNTABLE NOUN
Philanthropy is the giving of money to people who need it, without wanting anything in return.

power UNCOUNTABLE NOUN
If someone has **power**, they are able to strongly influence people and control events.

preach TRANSITIVE VERB, INTRANSITIVE VERB
When someone **preaches**, or **preaches** the **Bible**, he or she gives a talk on a religious or moral subject, usually as part of a church service.

preacher COUNTABLE NOUN
A **preacher** is a person who gives talks on religious or moral subjects, usually as part of a church service.

product COUNTABLE NOUN
A **product** is a substance such as lipstick or face powder which people use to make themselves look nicer or to improve the condition of their skin or hair.

programme COUNTABLE NOUN
A **programme** is a series of actions or events that take place over time and are intended to have a particular result.

pub COUNTABLE NOUN
In Britain, a **pub** is a building where people can buy and drink alcoholic drinks.

refinery COUNTABLE NOUN
A **refinery** is a factory where substances such as oil or sugar are processed from a basic state into a state that can be sold and used.

revolutionary COUNTABLE NOUN
A **revolutionary** is a person who tries to cause a revolution or who takes part in one, often using violence.

rival COUNTABLE NOUN
If people or groups are **rivals**, they are involved in the same sort of activity, and each is trying to do better than the other one.

set up (sets up, setting up or **set up) PHRASAL VERB**
If you **set up** a new company or other organization, you make all the arrangements for it to start to exist.

share COUNTABLE NOUN
The **shares** of a company are the equal parts into which its ownership is divided. People buy shares and usually receive some money every year in return.

skyscraper COUNTABLE NOUN
A **skyscraper** is a very tall building in a city.

slave COUNTABLE NOUN
A **slave** is a person who has to work without pay for someone who owns them.

slavery UNCOUNTABLE NOUN
Slavery is the system by which people are owned by other people as slaves.

social programme NOUN
A **social programme** is a series of actions or events that are intended to improve the lives of people in a particular place.

stable ADJECTIVE

1 If a substance or device is **stable**, it is not likely to change into a dangerous state.

2 If a situation is **stable**, it is not likely to become bad or unpleasant.

steam engine COUNTABLE NOUN

A **steam engine** is an engine that gets its power from steam. **Steam engines** are used to pull trains or to drive some machines in factories.

steel UNCOUNTABLE NOUN

Steel is a very strong metal made mainly from iron, and with some carbon.

strike COUNTABLE NOUN

When there is a **strike**, workers stop working for a period of time as a protest, usually to try to get better pay or conditions.

Supreme Court PROPER NOUN

In the United States, **the Supreme Court** is the most important court of law, which has power over all the other courts in the country and which can make a final decision.

telegraph UNCOUNTABLE NOUN

Telegraph is a system that uses electricity to send messages over long distances, usually along wires that connect two places.

tension VARIABLE NOUN

Tension is a feeling of fear and nervousness produced when people think that something bad or dangerous is likely to happen very soon.

tool COUNTABLE NOUN

Tools are simple instruments or pieces of equipment that you hold in your hands and use to do a particular kind of work.

trade UNCOUNTABLE NOUN

Someone's **trade** is the job that they do, especially when it is a job that needs manual skill that takes a long time to learn.

INTRANSITIVE VERB

When people or countries **trade**, they buy, sell, or exchange goods.

treat TRANSITIVE VERB

1 To **treat** someone or something badly means to behave towards them in a bad and cruel way.

2 When a doctor **treats** a person who is ill, he or she tries to make the person well again.

treatment VARIABLE NOUN

A **treatment** is a very thick liquid that you use to clean or protect your hair or skin and to keep it healthy.

Wall Street Crash PROPER NOUN
The Wall Street Crash was an event that happened in 1929 in the USA when the value of the shares of a lot of companies fell a long way. This led to a depression that lasted 10 years, during which many companies stopped working and many workers lost their jobs.

white settler COUNTABLE NOUN
White settlers were Europeans who came to live on the American continent, where the original people had a darker colour of skin.

Wild West SINGULAR NOUN
The Wild West is used to refer to the western part of the United States during the time when Europeans were first starting to live there. It is called wild because there were no laws and people used guns and violence to get what they wanted.

Collins
English Readers

AMAZING PEOPLE READERS AT OTHER LEVELS:

Level 1

Amazing Inventors
978-0-00-754494-3

Amazing Leaders
978-0-00-754492-9

**Amazing Entrepreneurs and
Business People**
978-0-00-754501-8

Amazing Women
978-0-00-754493-6

Amazing Performers
978-0-00-754508-7

Level 2

Amazing Aviators
978-0-00-754495-0

Amazing Architects and Artists
978-0-00-754496-7

Amazing Composers
978-0-00-754502-5

Amazing Mathematicians
978-0-00-754503-2

Amazing Medical People
978-0-00-754509-4

Level 4

**Amazing Thinkers and
Humanitarians**
978-0-00-754499-8

Amazing Scientists
978-0-00-754500-1

Amazing Writers
978-0-00-754506-3

Amazing Leaders
978-0-00-754507-0

**Amazing Entrepreneurs and
Business People**
978-0-00-754511-7

Visit **www.collinselt.com/readers** for language activities, teacher's notes, and to find out more about the series.

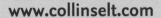